Authentic Content Marketing

Build An Engaged Audience
For Your Personal Brand
Through Integrity & Generosity

Second Edition

By George Kao
Authentic Business Coach
www.GeorgeKao.com

This is an unusual Copyright Information page...

I, George Kao, give you permission to copy/paste any part of this book and share it anywhere online or offline, as long as you adhere to the license below.

CC0 1.0 Universal (CC0 1.0) -- Public Domain Dedication
No Copyright

The person who associated a work with this deed has dedicated the work to the public domain by waiving all of his or her rights to the work worldwide under copyright law, including all related and neighboring rights, to the extent allowed by law.

You can copy, modify, distribute and perform the work, even for commercial purposes, all without asking permission.

In no way are the patent or trademark rights of any person affected by CC0, nor are the rights that other persons may have in the work or in how the work is used, such as publicity or privacy rights.

Unless expressly stated otherwise, the person who associated a work with this deed makes no warranties about the work, and disclaims liability for all uses of the work, to the fullest extent permitted by applicable law.

When using or citing the work, you should not imply endorsement by the author or the affirmer.

Read more about the license here:
https://creativecommons.org/publicdomain/zero/1.0/

It's important to me that these ideas get out into the world and implemented, so that we might see more connection, caring, and deep service in the business world.
--George Kao

Contents

Author's Note 1
    A Note for Paperback Readers 2
Introduction 3
Don't try to get attention. Be yourself and see who shows up 5
    Beware of typical marketing advice 5
    Your authenticity is greatly valuable 6
    Your ideal audience is seeking you 6
Your Content and Ads are a Ministry 8
    The Ripple Effect of Your Content 8
    Commit To Your Most Important Work 10
The Three Stages of Content 11
    Stage 1: Casual Content 12
    Stage 2: Improve on What's Liked 13
    Stage 3: Integrate & Productize 14
Four Ways I Overcome Creative Blocks 16
    1. Movement and Breath 16
    2. Remember Everything is a Draft 16
    3. Create Temporary Constraints 17
    4. Have a Conversation 17
The Five Success Factors for Content 18
    Demonstrate Your Care 18
    Choose Relevant Topics 19
    Discover Your Authentic Style 20
    Find Your Format 21
    Extend Your Reach 21
Why I don't protect my writings 23
    Why are you afraid of your content being used outside your control? 24
    You have unlimited ideas 25
Will Creating Free Content Get You More Clients? 27
    The Deeper Purpose of Creating Free Content 28
    Then how do we create content and make sales? 29

Create Your Content for One Caring Person...31
    Make your content for just one person at a time..............................31
Content Co-Working...34
Create First, Sequence Later..36
Free vs. Paid Content...38
    Teachers and Authors Deserve a Livelihood....................................38
    Relaxed vs. Studious..39
    Will Free Content Cannibalize Paid Content?...................................39
    Keep your free content "white belt"..40
    Zoomed-out Map or a Fun Small Section..40
    Free = What and Why. Paid = How..41
    Infotainment to Education to Transformation...................................41
Separate Your Content from Your Selling..43
    Phase 1: A pure focus on Selling..43
    Phase 2: Content Marketing...43
    Phase 3: Authentic Marketing...44
Authentic Social Media: Beware the Yearning for Validation.........................46
    Are you allowing social media engagement to influence your sense of self-worth?..46
    Your worth as a human being is unlimited.......................................47
    Authentic Expression..47
    So... should we NOT care about audience engagement?..............47
    Steps for Social Media Sanity:..48
Are you bothering people with your content?...50
    When you're of service, you're a blessing, not a bother..................51
Don't be afraid to lose people...54
Presence not Perfection...57
A Surprising Antidote to Content Perfectionism...60
Start Building An Audience Now— Even If You Have Nothing To Sell.........63
Let's Support Small Creators!..67
You Are Perfect Enough. You Know Enough. You Are Ready.....................71
Acknowledgements..74
About The Author...75

Author's Note

You can probably read this whole book in under an hour, and it might give you a good overview.

I also recommend re-reading it slowly, one chapter at a time, one day at a time. Glance through the Table of Contents, and when you find a topic that resonates, make it the only chapter you read for the day.

Take a few minutes to journal and reflect on how you can apply the idea to your own business.

At the end of each chapter, you'll find a link to the companion video. Whether or not you watch it, you're welcome to add a comment below the video. I'd love to know what you gained from the chapter, and any questions you have.

Let this book be a tool for you, a collection of ideas that, day after day, encourages and guides you into growing your authentic personal brand.

May you find purpose and joy in your work every day!

~ George Kao

A Note for Paperback Readers

Throughout the book, you will see some phrases underlined. These are hyperlinks and are clickable in the *electronic* copy of the book.

If you purchased a new copy of this paperback via Amazon, you can get the e-book (Kindle) version for free through Amazon's Kindle Matchbook program. Here's how:

1. Log into your Amazon.com account.
2. Search and find this book on Amazon.
3. Click on the Kindle version. If you purchased this paperback through your Amazon account, you should be able to get the Kindle version for free.

With the Kindle version you'll be able to click on the hyperlinks in this book.

Enjoy!

~ George Kao

Introduction

By Captain Orjiugo, Client & Mentee of George Kao

Wikipedia defines Content Marketing as "a form of marketing focused on creating, publishing, and distributing content for a targeted audience online."

Unfortunately, this definition does not do justice to content marketing as presented in this book by George Kao.

Beyond creating content just for the sake of "marketing", George has redefined content creation and distribution as a lifelong ministry and service of love to humanity.

Reading through this book will open up a whole new perspective for you, give you deeper reasons to let go of perfectionism, and inspire you to start sharing your views with the world as soon as possible.

As a successful business coach for more than 10 years, George walks his talk. He lives and breathes authentic content.

He is consistently blessing people all over the world with his kind and warm-hearted approach to business and marketing. Just look at his Facebook, Instagram, LinkedIn or Youtube.

I especially love this book for two reasons:

First, he's written it such that the chapters are independent of the others. So, you can read it through from beginning to end; or you can skip right to any chapter to learn a particular concept that interests you.

Second, the book is a perfect mix of mindset, inspiration, and real-life practice. You'll not only be inspired to start your own journey of authentic content marketing, you'll also get practical step-by-step mini-guides you can adopt right away.

Having observed George for several years, I am most honored to introduce the second edition of this book, Authentic Content Marketing.

Following his content approach has created unlimited opportunities for me as an Entrepreneur, and I have no doubt that it can do the same for you.

George is not one to promise results, and I respect him for that.

But I dare say that following the principles outlined in this book will yield immense benefits for your growth as a person; which will naturally translate to business growth and impact for your audience.

I welcome you to explore and enjoy this book, receiving it as the gift it was created to be.

May it help you on your journey towards a better business built on the foundation of true love, service, and dedication to your audience.

Captain Orjiugo
www.jacehr.com

Don't try to get attention. Be yourself and see who shows up.

In marketing, we typically learn about the importance of getting people's attention.

To try to stand out, to be more charming, to be more persuasive.

But that's not what I'm trying to do.

If anything, I'm trying to blend in. I know that my ideal audience will spot me, even in a sea of social media posts.

Being flashy tends to get unwanted attention. Irrelevant comments. More spam. It may seem like you have more followers, yet strangely, sales are still poor in your business.

Your audience may grow in the wrong direction, which increases your marketing costs over time, as it costs more to reach more people. Yet, you'll have to wade through the many fake followers to find and connect with your true fans.

When you try to get attention, it's unsustainable. People may find out how you are "normally" and become disillusioned, so you have to keep up a pretense to keep their attention.

A client of mine, with experience using visual interruption techniques ("pattern interrupt") to grow her audience, wrote:

"People who reply to the 'pattern interrupt' are maybe 80% the worst possible leads I've ever dealt with... if you have a hide like a rhinoceros and are willing to deal with lots of ugly, so you can finally hit the few good leads... it can eventually work. But is it worth it??"

Beware of typical marketing advice

Pay attention to the marketing teachings you're learning from. Notice how many marketers are in the energy of attention-grabbing.

Baiting their audience into watching or reading. Creating a presence that feels artificial and inflated.

These are normal behaviors in the online marketing world. They want us to believe that humans are constantly distracted and, therefore, require flashy and baiting tactics to finally pay attention... to "get them" to buy from us.

It's true that all humans are distractible. But, the more you assume they need flashiness to pay attention, the more you'll turn away your true fans.

And the ones who are left? They'll need you to be constantly impressive.

You'll end up behaving in ways outside your groundedness and personal truth.

Your authenticity is greatly valuable

Doing anything deliberate to try to get attention will take you out of your authentic energy.

Try to be less motivated by the thought of praise or purchases and, instead, explore how to resonate with your audience from a more authentic space.

If you practice simply being more deeply yourself, you will naturally be unique.

And you'll automatically be more attractive to your true fans.

We need to remember that **how we truly are** is of incalculable value to the people we're most meant to serve.

We simply need to show up daily with our authenticity.

Your ideal audience is seeking you

The truth is that your ideal audience is already looking for someone like you. They don't know what you look like, but they feel a resonance when they encounter you.

As an example, I often make text-only posts (it's mostly what I do on my FB page, see here: George Kao's Facebook Posts). Even though text-only posts might seem "boring" on Facebook, my ideal audience immediately has a feeling of recognition: "There's something deeply true about this message… let me keep reading."

I post videos that aren't edited. They're live videos which I do in a single take. Your ideal audience probably doesn't need you to edit much, if at all. However, if you *enjoy* editing your videos, go for it. Just be sure it's a process that's personally sustainable for you.

It's not that you should never be artful or entertaining. It's about doing it from your authenticity rather than any feeling of attention-seeking or desperation.

If you enjoy expressing beauty or humor, then do it! But don't *try* to be beautiful or funny. Be as if you were with a dear friend who accepts you completely. Yearn to connect your joy to theirs, your passion to theirs.

As you go about your marketing, consider the following questions:

- Are you enjoying the process?
- Are you tapping into the unconscious flow that comes from genuine expression?
- Are you compassionately serving your audience?

Keeping these questions in mind will help you to create without thinking about yourself and the praise you might get.

Take on an attitude of curiosity about who will resonate with you just as you are. Treat your audience like they accept your authenticity, and you will attract those who will do exactly that. By being yourself, marketing becomes less of a chore and turns into a beautiful form of self expression and exploration and service.

To watch the companion video or comment on this chapter, go here: http://bit.ly/acmv2c1

Your Content and Ads are a Ministry

No one in history has your exact combination of life experiences.

No one has the blend of challenges you've experienced, nor resolved them in your specific way.

No one has your unique voice, personality, and style, nor your combination of experience, skills, and passion.

There are people who will resonate with **you** and **your message** like nobody else they've ever encountered.

Your ideal audience is helped by you, in your area of expertise, more than they can be helped by anyone else.

To "minister" to someone is to serve their well-being. Your content and your ads can be a ministry. Here's how:

What if you shifted your mindset about content creation -- and running ads to promote your content -- from being a marketing chore, to being *a ministry in and of itself?*

When your content reaches your ideal audience, it blesses them.

Your content *is* a service in and of itself.

The Ripple Effect of Your Content

The change that your content helps someone to make, ripples out and blesses the people in their lives as well.

In the topics you love helping people with, there are thousands (perhaps millions) of individuals who will be profoundly changed by your story and message. They are struggling in life, or they've hit a wall, and your content might just be the key that unlocks a new door for them.

Who knows? Maybe your content, in reaching your ideal audience, makes as big a difference as any effective charity. Sure, it'll be hard to measure in terms of lives saved or houses built, but then again, how does one measure the ripple effect of **a heart transformed**, or **a mind changed**?

When people start to treat themselves and the people around them with greater love and wisdom, it goes on to create more profound changes than you can imagine.

Consider this possibility -- your most effective volunteer hours, and your most effective charity dollars, might be to get **your unique message** to the people who need it most.

This is why I preach the message of authentic, relevant, consistent content: some people need your help more than anything else. The unique combination of your experiences and voice resonates deeply with them.

Think of the act of reaching your ideal audience—those who are most helped by you—as a mission, a cause, a ministry.

The quickest way to reach your ideal audience is through boosting your content through paid ads.

My favorite method is Facebook Ads because it's smart enough to help you find the thousands of people most likely to engage with your content, i.e. the people who can most be helped by you. (Note: I teach a related online course: Facebook Ads for Authentic Marketing.)

What if buying Facebook Ads for your content, to reach and help your ideal audience—without any attachment to them buying from you—is one of the most beneficial ways to spend your "charity" dollars? What if you ran ads with the sole intent of providing content to the people your content can bless?

Whichever kind of paid ads you run to promote your content, don't look at it as just another marketing channel, but as an act of service.

Commit To Your Most Important Work

Commit to creating your content passionately, authentically, consistently -- as an act of service to your ideal audience. Buy ads to spread that content to the thousands who need your help.

Of course, when more of your ideal audience consumes your content, more of them may want to engage with your paid services or buy your products. If so, your business will fulfill its mission even more.

However:

Have no attachment to whether or not they buy from you.
Keep a higher intention of helping, of service, of love.

In this way, you'll infuse your content with more heart and, by removing any attachment to any specific profit, you'll prevent potential resentment.

Occasionally observe your stats to see what content is helping your audience the most, by seeing which content they engage with. This will inspire you to make additional relevant content that will serve their growth.

Allow the money-making (and even their appreciation of you) to be a byproduct -- a delightful surprise -- rather than what you're entitled to.

This way, as you do your marketing actions with a heart of service, you are doing authentic marketing!

To watch the companion video or comment on this chapter, go here: http://bit.ly/acmv2c2

The Three Stages of Content

There's a common mistake that I see from aspiring content creators. Maybe you have done this, too:

You have an idea that inspires you... so you think that it must excite other people, too. Understandable!

Therefore, you put lots of time (and maybe money) into packaging that idea into a book... or a course... or you create an amazing video, and after a lot of hard work, you share it with the world... and you wait.

What usually happens?

There's far less response than you hoped for...

Why does this happen?

You just fell for a core human bias -- to be inside your own head. You neglected to **adequately test** the idea to see if it truly resonates with other people -- besides yourself -- before you spent all that effort.

Perhaps you think it's a visibility issue, so you try harder to promote it.

Still, the result is baffling: why is something that's obviously **so good** (in your mind) not a game-changer for others?

Why aren't people getting it?!

This may lead to feelings of resentment or cynicism.

If you keep experiencing this, you might even decide to quit altogether, believing that because you're not getting the response you had hoped for, that it's just "not your thing".

The key to overcoming this is to understand that:

No matter what, your passion *is* a good idea... but *how* you share it will determine the response.

You need to experiment with different ways of sharing the idea, in the mindset of testing, until you discover a way that you ideal clients easily "get."

In order to do this, I recommend using The Three Stages of Content approach.

Stage 1: Casual Content

This is where it all starts.

For example, I casually make three short videos while on my long Saturday walks with my dog. In each video, I share an idea that I think *might* be helpful to some clients and audience members.

In fact, this very chapter was inspired by one of those casual videos:

Video: 3 Stages of Content

Update: *By 2018, I've created so much content that, since then, most of my content creation is Stage 2 (I'll describe that later.) I still make a Stage 1 video each Friday, from my office, as it's become much easier to do that than making my dog walk videos.*

I have no expectations about how these casual videos turn out. At this stage, I spend as little effort as possible. Therefore, I am not concerned whether the content gets any likes or comments.

I need to make an important distinction here: I **care** about my audience. And I care about the practice of experimentation with Stage 1 Content. I don't concern myself with how people respond, because Stage 1 is meant to be exploratory and experimental.

The Principles of Stage 1 Content:

(1) Explore a new idea, or try a different way of expressing an old idea.

(2) Test the idea with the market by sharing it on social media, and have **zero expectations**.

(3) Minimize your energy and time when making Stage 1 Content, since you don't know if your audience will like it, no matter how im-

portant you believe the message to be. "Casual" is the word that helps me in this situation: relaxed and unconcerned; temporary or impermanent.

(4) Be **prolific** and **consistent** with your Stage 1 Content, so that you give yourself *many opportunities* to explore ideas and different ways of saying things, spending *as little energy as you can* for each piece. Remember, you are testing here, not trying to be perfect or polished.

In my definition, ***anything*** that is published **for the first time** is Stage 1 content, whether it took 5 minutes or 5 years to make. Stage 1 is all about the audience's feedback to something they're seeing **for the first time.**

I've noticed that *no matter how unpolished* my content is, the choice of topic -- or how I frame it -- makes all the difference for whether there is audience engagement.

Only if it gets good feedback from the audience do I then progress the idea to Stage 2.

Stage 2: Improve on What's Liked

Once a month or so, I recommend revisiting your recent Stage 1 content to see which pieces received the most likes, positive comments, or shares, especially from people who are your ideal clients.

It is these well-liked pieces that are worth the effort to bring into Stage 2.

Stage 2 is where you:

- Think about how the piece can be improved.
- Integrate any comments or feedback.
- Consider whether another story/example would make it more impactful.
- Think about whether the headline/title can be improved.

Once you've made your edits, **share the piece again**, this time with a wider audience.

Perhaps you casually shared the Stage 1 version on the social media platform you use often. Now, your Stage 2 version can be shared on all the social media platforms you use, as well as to your email subscribers. You should, also, consider using some advertising dollars to promote that content.

If you have any friends with an audience that might enjoy this re-edited piece of content, consider emailing it to them personally. Let them know that this had traction with your audience, and you made it even better, and would love to know what they think.

Besides improving and re-sharing, you might also consider re-purposing this content into another format -- for example, turn an article into a video, or a video into an article.

Stage 3: Integrate & Productize

Stage 3 is about creating something from your content that can add to your income and your legacy.

To do this, once every quarter, take a look at your collection of Stage 2 content. Identify how the pieces you have created can be categorized into themes.

You can then take one of the themes that emerge and consider turning the content into a product, such as a book or a course.

In fact, each of my books is a Stage 3 piece. It combines my Stage 2 posts into a themed and sequenced package, with a designed cover and table of contents.

--

Your content will have a much greater chance at success if you follow these three Stages.

Too many people ignore Stages 1 and 2 (or don't even realize they exist) and jump right into writing a book or creating a course, and are baffled when it's not successful.

It's also helpful to understand that what you see from others is often **their** Stage 2 or Stage 3 content. We generally don't notice people's

Stage 1 content because the social media algorithms and search engines only show us what's *already* getting above-average engagement.

And that's good news for us too. We don't have to be concerned that our Stage 1 content will get too much visibility because, if it isn't actually good, it will usually be buried by other people's Stage 2 content!

I hope this will encourage you to **try many ideas**, and discover what the world really needs from you.

By following these three stages, with a mindset of **playful experimentation**, you'll enjoy your creation process even more.

Now, go create some Stage 1 content with gusto! Be casual, be prolific, be experimental. And enjoy the process!

To watch the companion video or comment on this chapter, go here: http://bit.ly/acmv2c3

Four Ways I Overcome Creative Blocks

Creative blocks show up for me in different ways:

- I'm working on a project, I feel intimidated… and I don't know what to do next.
- I'm planning my content and no ideas are coming.
- I'm trying to solve a problem and I'm drawing a blank.

Here's what I do…

1. Movement and Breath…

Take a few seconds to stretch, breathing deeply, and giving thanks for the Love and Wisdom that is abundant here -- now -- and always available.

If needed, I'll get up and walk around the room. The stuckness begins to dissolve.

If I need more, I'll step outside. Stretch. Take a few more deep breaths. A minute later, I have newfound energy!

2. Remember Everything is a Draft…

Nothing I publish is meant to be perfect. I'm always posting the **next** version, knowing that I can always improve, and make a better draft in the future.

The most important thing is to publish, or complete, **this** version as soon as possible.

I apply this to projects both small and big and small: social media posts, as well as books and courses, too.

If something is especially helpful to people, I'll earmark it for a future update.

There's no failure. There's only "this version" and the desire to improve the next version. "Mistakes" are clear feedback of what I can do differently, perhaps better, next time.

3. Create Temporary Constraints...

If I'm trying to come up with blog ideas, I ask myself:
"If I could **only** write about three things, what must those three be?"

While I'm writing:
"If I could only describe three things about this topic, what must those be?"

If I'm stuck on a problem:
"If there were three solutions to this problem, what might those three be?"

If I'm procrastinating:
"What are the next three simple, baby steps I can take?"

4. Have a Conversation

Being stuck often has to do with "being in our own head".

If possible, get into a conversation with a trusted colleague.

If you have one, reach out to your life coach.

If these options aren't possible, send a quick message to a friend (or three!) Tell them you're stuck on something and see if they have any ideas, or if they can ask you any questions to help you get going again.

Try these methods the next time you're creatively stuck! You might surprise yourself with how quickly you get unstuck, and maybe even realize you weren't as stuck as you thought you were.

To watch the companion video or comment on this chapter, go here:
http://bit.ly/acmv2c4

The Five Success Factors for Content

To reach more people, and make a deeper impact with your message, work on improving these five factors in your content.

Use this list as an audit of your content marketing. Make gradual improvements and you'll see better results over time.

Demonstrate Your Care

How do you get your audience to care about your content?

By showing that you care about them.

As it's often been said, "People don't care what you know until they know that you care."

How can you demonstrate that you care?

By getting to know your audience more deeply.

In the first few years of my audience-building, I did a "fan interview" several times a month. (To this day, I continue to do about one every other month.)

This is where I reach out to an audience member (ideally, someone who has bought something from me, or otherwise has engaged a lot with my content) and have a one-on-one "meet and greet" conversation with them.

We split the conversation in half:

In the first part, I am asking them questions to help me understand:

1. What they've bought before in my industry -- things related to what I offer.
2. What else they've bought that's not in my industry, but related. For example, some type of coaching, consulting,

counseling, workshops, retreats, courses, books that are somewhat related to my topics.

3. Of the things they spent the most money on, what didn't work well, and why?
4. I then ask them to imagine a perfect support structure for them to grow (in the areas that I help people with). What might that support structure look like? (This helps me to shape my future offerings.)

The second half of the conversation is for me to help them with anything at this time. For example they can pick my brain for 15 minutes, or I can give them an experience of what I do.

Another way to better understand your audience is to look at their social media profiles and explore the items they are posting and sharing. This will show you what they care about right now. In other words, can you post things like that too? How might it influence or improve your content topics, format, or style?

You can also demonstrate care for your audience by engaging with their comments.

Through your actions, your audience, even if they're brand new to you, will be able to feel whether you really care, or are merely trying to get them to do something like opt in or buy.

Choose Relevant Topics

It doesn't matter how skillful you are as a writer, or how charismatic you are as a speaker, or how amazing your website looks. If **the topic** of what you're writing or speaking about isn't what your audience is looking for, you'll have a very hard time getting any traction.

By focusing on the topics that matter to them, you'll create content that they are looking for, **or** didn't know they needed, but once they encounter it, they will be so glad they found it.

Have you gotten to know your audience well enough to know what topics would excite or deeply interest them?

Even if you're not a skillful writer or speaker, the topic will save the day. You'll notice this as you browse social media: people often re-share things that aren't necessarily well-produced (though that doesn't hurt either!). They share posts on topics they care about.

If you have **already** been creating content, observe which of the posts you've made get the most engagement. Why not post more things on those popular topics?

Discover Your Authentic Style

Everybody has a different style, and that's a good thing.

Some people copy others' styles because it looks successful. This may work for a while, but you're likely suppressing your best authentic style. You'll also burn out, trying to pretend all the time.

Instead, commit to experimentation. Try different things so you can discover your authentic style and fully step into it.

Imagine being with an audience that completely supports you (in their eyes you can't do any wrong). How would you behave? What style of writing, or speaking would you employ?

It may help to imagine being with an unconditionally-loving friend, family member, or mentor. If you were talking with or writing to them, what would your style be?

This is an ongoing process to find and settle into your most authentic style.

For some people it's humor. For others, it's having a certain gravitas. Some people enjoy some formality in their communications. Others excel when they're casual.

Your style is your brand. What colors attract you? What personality are you when being your most natural and best self? What values do you love and champion?

The more you understand your authentic style, the more you can activate your unique superpower, and your ideal audience will find you naturally attractive.

Find Your Format

Your style will shine differently in different formats. It's up to you to experiment enough to discover your various strengths.

Give different formats an honest try before you judge whether it's for you or not:

Format	Guidelines
Videos	Long - more than 10 minutes Medium - 3-10 minutes Short - 30 seconds to 3 minutes For videos, you could try scripted vs. off-the-cuff
Blog posts	Long - more than 1,500 words Short - usually 300-700 words
Tweets	Up to 280 characters
Podcast	Audio only Long, medium, short You could try interviews vs. individual
Images	E.g. Instagram posts

You don't have to show up in every format. But it is wise to experiment with most, if not all. Then you can get a better feel for what you'd most like to get great at and continue practicing using those formats.

Someone might go viral being on Twitter, whereas another person might do really well with writing very long blog posts. Another person might focus on making videos. There's not one format that is meant for everyone!

Extend Your Reach

Without understanding the strategy of reach, it will be very hard for your content to find its way to your ideal audience. You might as well be writing in a private journal, or making videos only for your clients (both of which can be great ways to start, by the way!)

My two favorite ways to reach more people are:

- Ads on social media platforms - for example Facebook and Instagram. This is perhaps the easiest way to reach the greatest number of people, in a highly targeted way. Many marketers agree with me. You can learn these by watching Youtube videos for free. If you'd like to learn my strategies step by step, take one of my courses: www.georgekao.com/workshops

- Collaborations. Get started by reaching out to a peer that you resonate with, or someone who has a similar audience as you. Trade content promotions with each other: you'll share one of her best posts with your audience and she'll do the same for you. If your audiences are similar in character and size, it will be a win-win for everyone.

There are many other ways to grow reach -- SEO, Google Ads, speaking on podcasts, Amazon Ads, to name a few.

**

Your potential is beyond what you can imagine. There's no top level for these improvements for your content marketing -- it's an ongoing journey and opportunity for growth. With baby steps, you can make improvements in each of these five areas, and increasingly fulfill more of the mission of your purpose and your business.

To watch the companion video or comment on this chapter, go here: http://bit.ly/acmv2c5

Why I don't protect my writings

I don't worry about anyone -- or any company -- repurposing my content or using it in whatever way they want.

This sounds bold, but it actually gives me peace of mind and inspires more creativity.

Disclaimer: This may not be the right legal advice for you, so please do your own research before deciding to uncopyright as I've done.

Recently there's been some uproar in the Medium.com community around their updated terms of service. Even before they added clarifications, I was perfectly fine with the updates.

In essence, Medium can use the writings of their members -- without compensating the writers.

Seems terrible, right? Why would anyone want their writings to be uncompensated?

Those who are fearful or angry are making some assumptions:

1. That it's possible to make more than a few dollars a month from monetizing our blog writing. (Very rarely is that the case.)
2. That having one's writing get distributed widely -- especially without compensation -- is *a bad thing* if one can't control it.

As a business coach, I think these assumptions are based on misunderstanding the *real* potential of one's writing.

Here's what I've learned from ten years of building a successful **content-based** solopreneur business, and coaching hundreds of others to do the same:

1. The more widely your content is spread -- which will be mostly outside your control if it's to spread widely -- the bigger your audience will be.

2. The bigger your audience, the easier it is for you to sell *anything* (other than books) to make real, worthwhile money.

3. Whether you sell your own products and services, or make commissions selling others' products, the sky's the limit when you have a large enough audience.

Why are you afraid of your content being used outside your control?

If someone is going to distribute your content, it's because they're impressed enough to spread it!

What about people taking credit for *your* content, calling it their own?

1. It rarely happens. My content has been uncopyrighted since 2014 (here's a 2020 restatement of my uncopyright), and I have only seen a few isolated instances of people taking my content and calling it their own. It's truly rare, and I don't worry about it at all.

2. Even when they try to take credit for it, "their" stolen content doesn't spread, because it's *not their* usual voice. Readers sense it pretty quickly.

Very importantly, when you post something online first, it means that there will always be a timestamp for when that original content was *first* published on the internet. That means you'll always be able to claim that you were the first, if you ever need to do that. (I've never needed to.)

(To get a timestamp, it's best to post that content on Youtube or Facebook. With Youtube, one can't edit the original video, so it's a confirmed timestamp. With Facebook, make a video sharing the idea (simplest) or write a text-only post, which you can still edit in the future but the original version is still time stamped and publicly available one clicks the 3 dots of that post and click "View edit history.")

This is why I make it an urgent priority to publish content as quickly as possible. I prefer to be the first at sharing an idea, because I don't want anyone to think that I took it from them.

And yet, anyone is welcome to take my content and call it their own, or modify it as their own. Like I said, over the years, this has only given me peace of mind and fueled my creativity.

You have unlimited ideas

If you believe that you only have a small number of ideas within you, you're limiting yourself greatly.

The Truth (with a capital T) is that your potential for creativity -- and the variety of ideas you could come up with in your lifetime -- is truly unknown. It is quite vast, especially if you practice creating consistently!

The more you create (the more content you produce) the more you'll realize you have even more to say.

The more that your content is spread out there, by you, or by someone else, or by some social media platform, the larger your audience will be.

The larger your audience, the more monetization opportunities you'll have. *Even the people who are telling you that you can make money writing are making most of their money selling online courses about how to make money writing!*

We no longer have to wait for anyone (for example, a respected publisher) to choose us, to promote our work.

We can take our destiny into our hands. Self-publish.

I put all my writings into the Creative Commons (specifically, creative commons zero, but you don't have to be that hardcore, as there are many creative commons licenses).

Even though publishers won't want to publish my existing creative-commons books, they might contract with me to write a future book that they own the rights to… that is, if I allow them to ;-)

In summary, liberating my content from copyrights has grown my audience and made me much more creative. I now have more ideas than I could possibly write or create in a lifetime. That, and more peace of mind.

To watch the companion video or comment on this chapter, go here: http://bit.ly/acmv2c6

Will Creating Free Content Get You More Clients?

*"Just unsubscribed from a group which I had been a member for only 3 months. She was sharing free content, along with a few live videos. Eventually, she posted that **people are taking advantage, not hiring her as a coach after consuming her content.** Literally she said 'If you don't want to move forward, just leave.' So I left, because I sensed anger and lack."*

--a comment posted on my FB page.

First of all, I have to say that I can relate to both sides: the client, and the coach.

I've been there—thinking that just because I've shared a lot of free content with my audience, that I'm *entitled* to have them buy from me. When they didn't, I was resentful.

Resentment builds when we *pretend* to be generous yet harbor an ulterior motive of expecting people to buy... and then discover that they have their own timing!

Instead, we thrive when we create free content as a **ministry** *and as an* **exploration** *of our own calling. (See Chapter 2.)*

In the *long*-term, you will get enormous benefits by being generous and service-oriented. But nobody - not even the smartest marketing expert in the world - can tell you **when** you can expect that return to be... or in what form.

If you build a genuine and loyal audience -- and you understand their wants and occasionally announce your aligned products/services -- you will tend to make sales or get clients... even with gentle launches, as I do.

However, please don't think of your content strategy mainly as a client-getting tool.

That's the problem I have with funnel-type of launches, e.g. create a free Facebook group for a 30-day challenge, and then try to convert them into buyers.

The participants innocently join what they perceive to be a wonderful free thing… yet the host has the ulterior motive of converting the members into buyers within a specific timeframe. In this case, almost everybody will experience some kind distrust or resentment.

It's been said that "Expectations ruin relationships."

I'll go further and say that *an attitude of entitlement will ruin the relationship with your audience.*

If you grow an audience, yet feel entitled to having them buy from you ("since I've given them so much already!") then your actions will tend toward manipulation, and erode the very relationship you hoped to build.

We are not entitled to anything, *not* to our audience's attention, let alone their purchases.

The Deeper Purpose of Creating Free Content

The deeper purpose of free content — a purpose you can feel great about — is to to **clarify** your own message and to **gather** and **serve** an audience of **kindred spirits.**

There is no "end" or final stage to that great purpose.

After having coached hundreds of content creators, I see that we can never one day "finally" have finished clarifying our message or exploring our voice.

It is an ongoing journey of deepening clarity, resonance, and precision.

You can never "finally" build an audience — your audience will continue to evolve. Some who are less aligned will leave. Other kindred spirits will find you. You'll keep being discovered by people who are resonant with you and your message.

Then how do we create content and make sales?

My advice to that resentful coach mentioned at the beginning (again, with whom I can empathize!) is the following:

1. Remind yourself of the deeper purpose of creating content. Make that purpose ingrained within yourself by reflecting on it —journaling, meditating, praying, or talking with a friend or coach about it. Feel the privilege you have to share messages that help others.

2. Then create and share your authentic free content consistently, in the spirit of exploration and service to your audience.

3. Make sure that your ideal audience is seeing your content. My favorite techniques for reaching audiences are with FB/IG Ads and authentic collaborations. (I teach courses on these outreach strategies.)

4. As you start to gather an audience that engages with your content, recognize how lucky you are that these people are willing to *pay you* their precious attention. There are so many articles they can read, millions of videos they can watch, or podcasts they can listen to. The spending of their time is the **one currency** that they won't get back. Appreciate your audience's attention. Feel and express your gratitude for them.

5. Get curious about what your audience wants from you. Notice what pieces of content they respond to, and create more like that. Do this to serve your audience, and as a project of further exploring your Calling—that blessed intersection between your passions and what your audience wants.

6. Talk to your audience about what services, products, and programs they have bought, and what they are looking for. What have they bought -- related to what you might offer -- that didn't satisfy them? What are they still seeking that they can't find? *Recognize how fortunate you are to have an audience that you can talk to, for clarifying these things.* This kind of market research is incredibly valuable.

7. Create those services/products/programs that they seek. Alternatively, you can also find another seller who provides those, and earn a commission in sharing those products with your audience.

Keep repeating these seven steps. You'll grow a true audience and come to deeply understand them. This allows you to build a successful, authentic business.

Remember, your audience isn't there just to buy from you.

You are blessed to have an audience, no matter how small at the moment.

Over time, you'll grow your audience and eventually, you'll have plenty of grateful clients as well!

Just don't be fixated on an exact time it "should" happen.

I'll close with a quote from a reader of mine who commented on the post that became this chapter:

"Creating authentic free content is a wonderful lesson on humility, abundance and service."
-- Annie LM

To watch the companion video or comment on this chapter, go here: http://bit.ly/acmv2c7

Create Your Content for One Caring Person

Many of the blocks to creating content can be solved by one mindset shift:

Make your content for just one person at a time.

Don't write for "the world".

Don't make videos for "your audience."

That kind of approach can cause performance anxiety, which blocks you from showing up consistently.

Instead, imagine that you are talking to just one person… someone you feel comfortable talking to, someone who loves your ideas.

It might be an ideal client, a kind friend, a supportive colleague, or a true fan. Someone who can't wait to hear from you.

What might they want to know about your area of expertise?

Create a piece of content with only them in mind.

After you've created the content, share it with them: "I was thinking of our conversation, and made this… let me know if you find it helpful or have any questions!" The usual response is that they'll feel honored and cared for.

If they find it helpful, ask them if they would feel OK if you shared it more widely -- assuming that in your content, you didn't mention any personal details about them.

Once they give you permission, post it on your social media. It will help others who have similar challenges!

The benefits of this method:

1. You'll reduce your performance anxiety by being in conversation with only one person, someone who already likes you.

2. That one person feels special that you made content with them in mind.
3. If you share it on social media, that piece of content will attract and resonate with others who are like them. This will grow and nurture your ideal audience.

Do you already work with clients? Start practicing this -- carve out five minutes after each client session to jot down a quick note. What was the client's core problem or question? Did they have an "aha!" moment in the session? These are content ideas that could be relevant to your audience too!

Do you get questions via email? Email a thoughtful response to your client. If they find it helpful, transform that into a blog post!

Video instead of email. Try this: instead of writing, record a short video to respond to your client (without mentioning their name). You can start the video saying, "So the question is XYZ and here are my thoughts about it...." (so that you keep their name out of the video). See if your client finds it helpful. If so, ask them if it feels appropriate for you to share the answer publicly so others can benefit.

No clients yet? Then make some time to talk with a friend and have them ask you questions about your work and your core message. If you're both comfortable, record that conversation so you can speak without having to take notes. Your answers can be turned into one (or more) new pieces of content!

I enjoyed reading this public speaking book: *Be Heard Now* by Lee Glickstein. (I've linked you to the Audio version -- the author reads the book in his compassionate voice.)

The advice I remember most: when speaking on stage, don't look at the "overall" audience, trying to take them all in. Instead, find one welcoming face in the audience and look at them, talking as if only to them for 15 seconds. Then, find another welcoming face and talk to them for another 15 seconds. And so forth, connecting with one person at a time.

Of course, those individuals you connect with will feel appreciative that the speaker is looking at them. They'll brighten up, which positively affects those around them. It uplifts the speaker too.

What's magical is that *the whole room* will feel the connection you are having to that one person. The fact is that **you are more resonant when you are talking heart to heart**, mind to mind, being in relationship with just one being. You're natural, conversational, and authentic.

I also heard that this is how Tim Ferris wrote *The Four Hour Workweek*. At first, he wrote it as a "book", but disliked the formality and deleted the draft! Then, he wrote it as if writing an email to a *specific* friend... and it became the book that made him famous.

When I first shared this a few years ago, one of my readers, Trevor Sutton, commented:

"I recall the exact advice given to me some years ago when I had the pleasure of presenting live Jazz programs on radio. Our trainer emphasized 'speaking to one familiar person, not everyone out there in Radio Land'. It worked. My thought patterns changed and my voice came over as more personal. Many audience members would meet me in the street and say that they felt they knew me well."

Another commenter wrote:

"I know from experience whenever I put this into practice, it works so well. Writing gets easier, connection becomes established, and courage is in flow!" -- Susanne Dahl

So make your content for just one caring person at a time.

Then share it publicly so others just like them can benefit!

To watch the companion video or comment on this chapter, go here: http://bit.ly/acmv2c8

Content Co-Working

"*When I am delivering a webinar or talking with clients, I show up with warmth, presence and the intelligence that the situation requires... but when I am creating content on my own — blog posts, videos — it's as if I don't know anything anymore. What can I say? Will they like it? ...and other doubts appear.*"

--a reader sent in this question, but I bet many of you can relate.

Try Content Co-Working:

Find a fellow content creator and arrange a one hour Zoom meeting. (Seeking someone? Add a comment below this post.)

STEP 1:

Start the session by having each of you talk casually for 5 minutes, regarding what you each wish to blog about in this hour.

STEP 2:

Open a new google document: www.doc.new

Turn on the Voice Typing feature... it's in the Menu under Tools... so that it will automatically transcribe whatever you say next.

STEP 3:

Start the zoom recording.

Set a 10-minute timer.

Speak to your friend about your blog post idea.

STEP 4:

Stop the recording.

Allow your friend to record and speak their ideas for 10 minutes.

(After the meeting is over, each person's recording will be on their own computer.)

STEP 5:

For the final 30 minutes, you can each edit your own voice transcript into a blog post.

If there's time, spend a few moments brainstorming titles for the post, and getting your friend's feedback.

**

That's it! Give it a try.

It's a fun way to create content :)

Want to find a content co-working buddy? Comment here: http://bit.ly/acmv2c9

Create First, Sequence Later

Don't be concerned about the sequence of what you create. No matter how much you plan, it is going to change.

Here's my experience after making 1,000+ videos, 4 books, and 20 online courses:

People don't consume content in the order that we hope they will. They usually just go to our most recent pieces.

Your ideal audience will be intrigued by your energy/presence, no matter which article or video they start with. If they're meant to be true fans, they will seek more from you.

But is there ever a time to sequence your content?

Yes. Just not at the beginning.

Remember the 3 stages of content? (Refer to Chapter 3.)

The 1st stage of content -- anything new -- is exploratory.

The 2nd stage -- improve on what has received above-average engagement.

The 3rd stage -- the integration & monetization of your best content.

It's in the 3rd stage that you finally create a sequence.

Therefore, at the start, simply put all of your ideas out there on social media, one by one, without concern about the sequence of the overall picture. Let the audience give you initial feedback as they see each of your pieces.

Once you notice which of your ideas gets traction, **then** improve and reshare it.

Eventually go to Stage 3 -- put things into a Book or Course, in the right place.

For example, this chapter you're reading started as an article. I probably should have written and shared it years before, but I put this out there as soon as I realized that people had questions about it. Once I saw the reactions to it -- that many people found it helpful -- I shared it again.

Now this "article" has become a chapter in this book!

Another important reason not to "sequence" too early is that any piece of free content should stand on its own, because people don't consume your content in the order you hope.

It takes practice to chunk down your knowledge into a single blog post that is understandable by itself. Trust that your intended audience has enough background knowledge to understand what you're saying.

It's also best to keep content in small digestible chunks. You will notice even within this book, I keep the chapters and even the paragraphs short.

Just let the audience ask you questions if they have any. You don't have to define everything in advance. It's ok to leave a little mystery!

You can also mention (or link to) another post or video that you have, if they'd like to explore more. However, assume that most people won't.

Again: just start creating. Practice packaging your knowledge into bite-sized chunks. Sequence later.

Dedicate yourself to consistent creation, and you'll get lots of needed practice!

To comment on this chapter, go here:
http://bit.ly/acmv2c10

Free vs. Paid Content

Which of your content should be free versus paid?

This is an important question which I will address in the second half of this chapter.

First, we need to talk about whether content **should** have a fee attached. For example: online courses.

I used to promote the idea that **all** content should be free because it would help humanity progress faster, help you attract your ideal audience, and make you more creative by easing the pressure in creating your perfect content.

A few years later, I changed my stance. Here's what I now believe:

Free content is beneficial. We're all thankful for Wikipedia, as well as the billions of free blogs and YouTube videos!

However, **paid** content is also important for the advancement of society...

Teachers and Authors Deserve a Livelihood

If you give all of your content away for free, you lose out on a substantial income source. You would need a job, which consumes hours every day, some of which you could've spent creating more and better content.

Not having a job is how I've been able to write so many articles and make videos to share freely -- to benefit people no matter if they ever buy from me. My business also frees up several hours every week to keep improving my paid courses.

Think about the writers and video creators you admire. Don't you wish they had more energy and time to create or improve their content? They need an income source that liberates them to do this.

That's why I promote the idea of supporting small creators.

Now let's talk about how the student of content relates to free versus paid.

Relaxed vs. Studious

Divide your content into two buckets -- **easy** for the reader versus **challenging**.

Most of the time, when people consume free content, they're relaxed and in "free time" mode, not looking to be so serious at the moment. They are seeking something entertaining that *also* brings them some value.

Therefore, free content should be **easy to consume**, nothing complex. It shouldn't require much investment of energy from the reader, just like it doesn't require any investment of money.

If you create a **challenging** piece of content that requires some study and energy to parse and understand, then the reader should spend *some* money (doesn't have to be a lot) to signal to themselves that they are ready to do the work, not only consume free infotainment.

Still, I believe that paid content should be as affordable as possible, since it is a scalable (ever expandable) revenue source. Make it accessible in price. Students don't have to invest thousands of dollars to show their willingness to do the work. But it helps if they pay a reasonable amount.

Will Free Content Cannibalize Paid Content?

I've discovered that even with lots of free content, my audience still buys paid information products, because it's more thoughtfully organized than the free stuff.

For example, the chapters of all of my books are freely available on my blog and social media, if you were willing to go through years of my videos and posts.

However, in my books, you get them in a sequenced and edited format.

Many others also do this. Prolific content creators Seth Godin and

Gary Vaynerchuk sell books that are essentially a curated collection of their best free content. And their books sell very well.

There are people like Seth, Gary, and me in every industry, including yours.

The more free, good content you create and distribute online, the more people discover you and will buy your books or courses.

Keep your free content "white belt"

Think of a martial arts dojo.

In any given beginner (white belt) class, you see a few dedicated "black belt" students practicing the same basic moves, except that the black belts are practicing at a deeper, more nuanced level.

Advanced students know how important the basics are, and they review them frequently.

Therefore, make most of your free content "white belt" because even "black belt" audience members will appreciate beginner's content. They'll notice deeper nuances than what beginners see.

In regards to your "black belt" content -- the more in-depth, complex, or difficult knowledge -- keep them in your paid courses, workshops, and books.

Once students have paid something, they're more ready to get serious and invest the required energy to parse and understand your more detailed or advanced material.

And, you're more ready to support them to go deeper.

Zoomed-out Map or a Fun Small Section

Another way to think about your free content is that it's either a zoomed-out map, or a fun detailed small popular section of town.

A zoomed out map gives them a quick overview of the landscape, illustrating where they are (their current problems, issues, situation, challenges, yearnings) compared to where they want to go (their dreams achieved, their challenges overcome.)

Sometimes, however, you may want to give, for free, a fun small section of the map, a popular part of town, for example, with some detail but keeping it easy to consume.

Your premium content, however, is the comprehensive and detailed map that connects everything together, and leaves no question about how to get from point A to B, including the helpful detours they might take, what they need to prepare for the journey, the pitfalls to avoid, and so on.

If you offer 1-1 services, this can be the GPS that leads them in a customized way.

Free = What and Why. Paid = How.

Another way of saying it is that your free content gives the What (the definitions and the philosophies) and the Why (the diagnosis of their problems, as well as the background of your philosophies.)

Your premium content gives the detailed step-by-step: How to solve their problems or reach their goals.

For example, in my free content I often talk about the importance of Facebook Ads, but it's in my paid course on Facebook Ads that I go into detail of how to do it efficiently and effectively.

Infotainment to Education to Transformation

Remember: when people are consuming free content, they're usually looking for some kind of picker-upper, something to entertain, inspire, uplift, give them energy and easy ideas. In other words, **infotainment**.

When they're ready to really solve a problem or achieve a dream or study something in a step-by-step way, then they're ready for premium content such as an online course. Now they're looking for real **education**.

Sometimes they can apply the education on their own. Other times, they would really benefit in working personally with the teacher, in a coaching or mentoring program. That's usually where the deepest **transformation** happens.

Now it's your turn -- What content might you offer for free, versus paid?

To watch the companion video or comment on this chapter, go here: http://bit.ly/acmv2c11

Separate Your Content from Your Selling

"Always aim at complete harmony of thought and word and deed. Always aim at purifying your thoughts and everything will be well."
— Mahatma Gandhi

This is where so many of us heart-based entrepreneurs fall down: we try to mix our selling with our moments of content generosity. We know it doesn't feel totally right. We may even sabotage our own efforts.

I recommend that we **separate our content from our selling.**

For some context, allow me to share what a 3-phase evolution that I've experienced in my own online marketing journey.

Phase 1: A pure focus on Selling

It's clear what the sales person is trying to do. Their primary purpose -- transparent to them, and to you -- is to sell you a product.

They might say they want to help you, but you know (and they know) that it's a byproduct of the main intention: to make sales.

If they're an ethical salesperson, they will do a good job of "filtering" or "qualifying" which is to ask good questions and help you explore whether the product is actually a good fit for you, that it will solve the problem you actually care about, and that it's the right timing for you to buy it.

Phase 2: Content Marketing

The blogger, podcaster, social media maven, especially if they're very heart-centered, might feel conflicted about Selling/Enrollment. They know they "have" to eventually sell, to stay in business, but they would prefer to simply give helpful content.

They may have learned from other marketing "experts" to create a "marketing funnel" where someone comes in at the top of the funnel through free content, then moves "down the funnel" to more in-depth content, then to a cheap product, then to more expensive products.

The problem with the Content Marketer is that they're sometimes conflicted internally.

Whenever they create content, they also have this (subtle) hope that their content will also eventually produce sales.

That internal conflict does not liberate the full creativity and effectiveness of **helping** that full altruism does.

Phase 3: Authentic Marketing

This is what I've been exploring for the past few years through my articles and videos.

I aim to borrow the best of Phase 1 and 2, and bring purity of heart and intention to the doing of each activity.

We understand that we have 2 separate activities in our business: (1) Selling and (2) Content.

It's like a business having 2 arms: the for-profit arm and the non-profit arm.

In each department, there is purity of intention. There is no psychological conflict. In this way, both can be done ethically and effectively for its purpose. You can make enough money, and yet also fulfill your natural desire to give and help with a full heart.

The key is that when I'm creating content, I'm not hoping that you'll buy anything from me. Occasionally in various blog posts I do link to courses that I sell, but it's more as an FYI, rather than pressuring my blog readers to buy.

Yet, I also consistently announce my launches and sales. When I sell, I aim with pure intention: I'm telling you why I created this product, who it's for, what it aims to help you with, and other details. My selling is not hidden within an article or video that purports to be free content.

To summarize, here are the benefits of separating content from selling:

- You feel the freedom to fully explore ideas that intrigue you, without feeling like you have to "perform" and sell effectively.
- You feel the abundant opportunity to experiment with finding your public "voice" and building confidence (and authority) with it.
- You don't feel like you're tricking the audience, pulling them in with "free" content only to have them experience a sales pitch at the end.
- If you are distributing your content, using Facebook or Instagram ads, for example, to increase the reach of your content, some of it will be shared widely, thus growing your audience.
- Some of your audience will then check out your services or products, and buy when it's the right time for them.

It's a natural byproduct of authentic marketing that people will eventually buy from you. "Making" people buy from you is not something you need to focus on.

Instead, focus on doing these two activities with pure heart -- content generosity, and selling with integrity -- and the business will tend to grow as well.

To watch the companion video or comment on this chapter, go here: http://bit.ly/acmv2c12

Authentic Social Media: Beware the Yearning for Validation

Most of the time, you do *not* get as much engagement on social media as you see other people get.

Why is that? Is it because people don't like you as much?

That's absolutely not the reason. The reason is how the algorithm works. When you browse the newsfeed or home screen of a social media platform, you only see the *tiniest* percentage of posts that *already* received more engagement than the average. (Engagement being likes, comments, and shares.)

In other words, social media only shows you the tip of the iceberg, a few of the most popular posts, and you *do not* see the vast majority of posts that have near-zero engagement.

You have to understand that **getting little engagement is *normal* for everyone except celebrities.**

Statistically, *most* of our posts are going to get less engagement than what we see others post. If we use the newsfeed (what we are shown due to algorithms) as our measuring stick, we'll be constantly discouraged!

This brings up several important issues.

Are you allowing social media engagement to influence your sense of self-worth?

"I often say that Facebook stokes our early attachment wounds." -- Carissa Lane

If you don't pay attention to this, you'll easily make the false connection:

"If I get more likes or comments, it means I'm more worthwhile."

With a moment of reflection, you can see how untrue that statement is.

Your worth as a human being is unlimited.

(Or if you believe there's no self, then there's no *self-worth* either!)

Most of the time we forget this, because society keeps us measuring our self-worth based on external approval.

Let me be one voice to remind you -- detach your social media engagement from anything having to do with how valuable you are.

Authentic Expression

When we forget about authentic expression, we lose our groundedness, our authentic power: *being able to express ourselves free of attention-seeking.*

When you're ungrounded from your authentic power, the world loses a moment of unique creativity from you.

It's an important practice, something I hope you'll do everyday -- to express yourself in connection to your deep, resonant truth.

You may find yourself *ahead of your time*. Many people won't understand you. That's ok. You've still added a piece of uniqueness in the world that will be appreciated in the future.

Sometimes, though, it just happens that an authentic expression of your deep truth **also** happens to resonate with others. In those moments, you get lots of likes, comments, or shares. Let this kind of generous engagement be a pleasant surprise rather than a consciously-manipulated result.

So… should we NOT care about audience engagement?

I wouldn't say that. It's about a difference of intention:

The conventional way -- "I'm unaware that I'm attaching my self-worth to the social media status I get, and so I'll study how others are getting engagement and emulate the tactics of popularity, in hopes that I also get more engagement. When I don't, I'll feel discouraged or resentful, and either quit, or use more persuasion methods."

The *authentic* way -- "On social media, I will practice mindfulness, knowing that it's easy to attach self-worth to likes, so I'll practice connecting to my source of infinite worth, and **then** create content from that authentic space. If it happens to resonate with others, what a delightful surprise! But either way, I'll keep practicing authentic connection and creation."

Continuing with the authentic way:

On an occasional basis (such as once a month), notice which of the content pieces you created got more engagement than usual. What topic was it? Or how did you approach that topic? And do you feel inspired, and in service, to create more content like that? If so, create more like that! But not until you first reconnect with your Source of worth, so that you can create from authentic expression, not because you expect another homerun.

Steps for Social Media Sanity:

1. If you haven't already, turn off notifications on your phone for likes/comments/shares.

2. Before you post, reconnect for a moment with your Source of infinite worth, or whatever you need to remind yourself that *you are not posting to get people's approval.*

3. Practice expressing / writing / recording from your authentic self.

4. Once you post / publish, **go do something else.** Don't keep checking to see if there is engagement! (This practice of ignoring the engagement will strengthen better boundaries. It increases your authentic power.)

5. Check the engagement once in a while. The purpose is seeing what Topic or Approach resonates with your audience. If there's little engagement, just remember: by creating, you are

practicing expressing yourself, and that itself is valuable. The time for results will eventually arrive. That is certain.

6. If there happens to be good engagement on something, consider distributing that content more widely, such as through Facebook or Instagram ads.

7. See it all as a long term journey of market testing and **nothing** to do with how valuable you are as a person. It's also no judgment on your skills, because you will keep improving if you keep creating!

8. One final thing. Don't ask friends to "like" your stuff, as this just creates more desperation!

Keep following these steps, and you **will** eventually build a true fan base who respond eagerly to just about everything you post!

Until then, embrace these words from Baz Lurhmann: "The race is long but in the end, it's only with yourself."

To watch the companion video or comment on this chapter, go here: http://bit.ly/acmv2c13

Are you bothering people with your content?

Do you ever feel like you're bothering people, when you share your content?

A participant in one of my workshops wrote:

"Consistency of communication is my goal. To hold myself more accountable to this and get over the problem I have with feeling that I am bothering people by sending them content via email or other means, even if they have signed up for my list!!"

You have an audience because they want to hear from you:

- Your Facebook friends are interested in your opinions (believe it or not!)
- Your followers on social media **want** to hear about your business.
- Your newsletter subscribers look forward to your newest content!

You are not bothering people when you send content that they **expect** from you, at a **frequency** they expect.

If you haven't been sharing content, then do your best to start being consistent at a sustainable rhythm for you, and your audience will become accustomed to that rhythm.

They appreciate your content when you share with a positive intention:

- a spirit of helpfulness
- a desire to connect
- an intention to delight them

Why aren't you bothering your audience? Because they want content that's relevant to them -- that's why they're following you!

It helps to remember that:

1. **People are bored**, even if they're busy. At various times of day (and night), they're looking for something that might pick up their spirits, educate them, or entertain them... something that makes them feel, or makes them think.

2. **People are hurting** and looking for a solution from someone like you. If they're following your content, it means they're actively trying to heal a current pain (which you can help them with) or are at least interested in learning from you.

3. **People appreciate you.** They seek your perspective and they like your presence. Otherwise, they wouldn't still be following you!

Before you create, first bring to your mind and heart someone specific from your ideal audience. One of your favorite clients, or a frequent commenter on your posts.

- Can you see that person in your mind's eye? What would they love to know about your area of expertise?
- On that topic, can you guess what they might be feeling? (Are they scared, overwhelmed, excited, eager, etc?)
- What could you say that would be helpful to them?

By creating content with your ideal audience in your mind and heart, and what you know about their situation, you are being of service.

You genuinely wish to help them, connect with them, or delight them.

When you're of service, you're a blessing, not a bother.

It's also good to be aware of some basic etiquette around sharing content...

How often is too often?

- Email Newsletters — unless they requested a weekly email, I wouldn't recommend more than 2x a month. In my email newsletter signup I ask subscribers to choose monthly or weekly, so that I align expectations.

- Social Media — are you posting more often than most people? Generally, once a day on any platform is acceptable. Once a week is fine but harder to stay top of mind. The latest advice: posting too often on social media?

- Private Messaging — this could be direct messages on Facebook, Instagram or Pinterest. Text/SMS, a personal email, or a LinkedIn private message. Are you sending content privately to people who didn't ask for it? Definitely don't do it if they don't already know you. However, if it's friends, colleagues, or classmates, it's fine to privately send content that you know would be relevant to them, once every few months, but include a thoughtful note about why they specifically might enjoy that piece of content.

- Posting about your business — you can definitely post about your products occasionally, perhaps every 1 out of 10 posts. You could increase that to 1 out of 3-5 posts on your Facebook Business Page and anywhere else that clients and prospective clients eagerly follow your business.

Here is evidence that you are *not* bothering your audience:

- Email Newsletter — each time you send one, you get fewer than 1% of the recipients unsubscribing. If you get more than 1% unsubscribe, then either you aren't emailing them often enough (quarterly is too rare) or you're emailing them too often (not more than once every 2 weeks unless they signed up for a higher frequency.) Also, if you notice that your Open Rate is consistently decreasing over time, it means you need to improve your content. You're not bothering them, but you may be boring them.

- Social Media — if your follower count rises organically (without buying followers) then you're doing fine. However, if your content engagement isn't rising, then again, the problem is that you need to improve your content.

In summary, create content with your ideal audience in mind and heart, and share it with them at an expected frequency, and your content will be seen as a blessing!

To watch the companion video or comment on this chapter, go here: http://bit.ly/acmv2c14

Don't be afraid to lose people

Gary Vaynerchuk curses a lot in his videos. This turns off a lot of people. I used to dislike him a lot! Now? I'm a big fan.

Seth Godin, who has written thousands of blog posts, never includes any images. He even has typos in his posts. I've humbly emailed suggestions and he's very open about making corrections. He probably loses a lot of potential readers.

I ignored Seth for a long time, but kept hearing about him from trusted friends, so finally I started reading his blog, and became a huge fan.

Andrew Yang has so many political positions that even if you love a few of his policies, you might get turned off by another dozen. Yet, his following grows by the thousands everyday.

Despite their unpopular behaviors, these influencers have long-term, raving fans. They'll never be in want. They can sell just about anything and make plenty of money.

At a much smaller scale, compared to these giants, I too have a loyal base of true fans. Yet, I'm unpolished in my videos, I never try to be fashionable (not personally interested!), and sometimes I say things in my courses and content that turn off even my own fans. Yet, my fans keep coming back again and again.

There are many other content creators and influencers who appear as if they don't give a damn about other people's approval… and yet, they're doing well.

How is that possible? Isn't caring about approval and popularity the very thing that helps you to become famous and successful?

The path of popularity can always work but along the way, you lose your soul as you try to please people.

I've chosen -- or rather, I have to keep choosing every day -- **the path of authenticity**: to be myself and see who wants to come along.

Those who are turned off by me and my shortcomings? Not a problem. There are many other content creators they can go follow. Why should I be greedy and try to make everyone follow me and lose my soul in the process?

"Be yourself" is actually a journey.

For years, I've been on this journey of authenticity -- a process of exploration, experimentation, discovery of my voice and my ideas.

Because I "think" out loud in my videos, in an unpolished way, I'm sure this turns off a lot of people.

At the same time, the journey also **fascinates** my true fans. And aren't they the ones who matter the most?

Your true fans care about your journey. They love to see your development as you work things out.

Don't ever be afraid of losing anyone.
Be more concerned about losing your soul.

As you explore and experiment with who you really are, you'll naturally attract your true fans. Give yourself the permission to try things that feel like it *might* be YOU. As you discover what resonates deeply in you, **you become more powerfully you.**

Ironically, *not caring* about others' approval is what builds true fans online.

It's about **not** being afraid. And that is highly attractive.

Yet, the paradox is that if you *try* to be attractive, you become afraid.

Don't *try* to be attractive or popular. The thing that's worth making an effort is *showing up consistently*, in a spirit of experimentation and exploration of who you are.

Wrestle and journal publicly with your ideas, your experiences, your past, your future, your love for service, your heart for the world.

Now, to build an audience, it helps a lot to get skilled at distributing your authentic content, so that your true fans have a chance to find you.

My favorite way of content distribution is through Facebook Ads. (I teach an online course about facebook ads.) My second favorite way is through collaboration (I have a course on that too which you can check out here: The Netcaring Course.)

Once you're actively creating and distributing your authentic content (your public journaling), don't be afraid to lose anyone.

For any newsletter, you'll always have *some* people unsubscribe, or unfollow you on social media. Don't be afraid. They may be back one day.

Either way, what's **more important** is that being more powerfully YOU is what your soul needs and is called to do. It's also what will draw forth your true fans, who are the only ones that matter.

To watch the companion video or comment on this chapter, go here: http://bit.ly/acmv2c15

Presence not Perfection

"I'm not sure I can sustain a presence on social media, even if it's good for business... it feels exhausting to have to keep up an image of who I am. Or maybe I will run out of things to say."
--a reader.

I get it.

If I had to pretend to be someone I'm not, it would exhaust me too.

If I were thinking about all the future posts I would have to make, it's not sustainable either.

But I'm doing neither of those things.

Instead, I'm being authentically on social media who I am today, saying what I know now. I'm not worried about an image to upkeep, nor all the future posts I have to make.

Just today is all I can handle.

Authentic Social Media is like an Authentic Friendship

When you're with a real friend, you feel like you can be yourself. Sometimes you're funny. Sometimes you're boring. Some days you feel attractive and other days, not so much. A real friend accepts all of it, cares about you through thick and thin.

Similarly, when you are willing to create and distribute authentic content, you'll also develop an audience who likes you for just who you are.

With a friend, you don't feel like you have to always plan what to say, what order to say it in. You simply share what's on your mind today, and what you think your friend would enjoy now.

Same thing with authentic social media. Do less planning, and be more honest and helpful, in whatever ways you already know how to be.

The simplest way this has been said is by Gary Vaynurchuk:

"Document, Don't Create."

When coming from the mindset of having "to create", you think your content has to be some work of art, or a brilliantly written article, and that becomes intimidating and scary.

Instead, simply "document" your thoughts and your journey, without pretense. Sure, you might take a minute to reboot your energy before showing up, but you don't require the content to be polished, brilliant, or to go viral.

Right now, as I'm writing this, I can do this one of two ways:

Perfection vs. Presence

Method 1 -- "To Create Perfection" -- to put pressure on myself that "this MUST be really good before I publish it, that it has to address exactly what my ideal audience wants, and it needs to be eloquently written."

Method 2 -- "To Document the Present" -- to show up, as I am, with my current thoughts, with a heart of humble service, not expecting whether or not you will "like" it, but simply with the faith that it's important to say **what is true for me now**, believing that it may eventually benefit someone.

Trying to create perfection is not sustainable, and yet that is what keeps many people from trying. Perfectionism is continuous self-punishment, repeating the inner voice of a strict authority figure from your past.

It's time to let that go. Give yourself what you always deserve: Unconditional Love.

Start with a supportive group

If it's too much for you to "document" publicly, then create a small, private Facebook group. Invite a few supportive friends or colleagues (ask them first) to witness and encourage your experimentations in documenting your journey.

Once you feel comfortable posting there -- consistently -- perhaps after a few weeks or months, expand that circle.

Eventually, you will be willing to post more publicly.

What should you "document"?

Your journey is truly unique. No one else has lived the life that you have. No one has had your exact thoughts, or learnt life's lessons in the same way that you have.

It's important for you to share your unique journey. Simply document, rather than giving yourself the pressure to "create".

Just show up and share what's true for you now, what you believe might be helpful to others, what is surprising to you, what you are observing about your field, what's going on in your life that might provide insight for others, what your intuition is telling you now.

Answer any questions that others have asked you. Or ask your friends to come up with some questions to ask you about your work.

The key is to never try creating "perfect" content.

It is simply enough to show up and share where you are on your journey with us.

To watch the companion video or comment on this chapter, go here: http://bit.ly/acmv2c16

A Surprising Antidote to Content Perfectionism

When it comes to your content, there is a harsh truth which, at the same time, is strangely calming:

No one is going to remember *any* of your content, except the few pieces that are exceptional.

Honestly, we're all too busy. There's always another shining piece of content that will distract us right after seeing yours. We don't think about yours at all, unless it's awesome, or greatly offensive (which it won't be!)

Does this mean you should give up if you haven't created anything viral yet?

If that's the prescription, then *not a single artist or writer* would **ever** become successful.

Instead, reflect on the biography of successful artists and authors -- they just *kept creating and publishing* until they stumbled upon their hit song or best-selling book. And, they aren't concerned about making content that *isn't* good.

Look at musicians: they are only known for their popular songs. Nobody remembers their "bad" songs.

Same with authors: they're remembered for their best-selling novels, even if they wrote many books. Sometimes, they're only remembered for *a single quote!*

This principle also holds true on social media. The algorithms of Facebook, Twitter, Linkedin, and Instagram, only show you the popular stuff in the news feed. You rarely see the thousands of other posts that got few or no likes.

Search engines are the same way: If people love a webpage, they will link to it and Google will bump it up in the search rankings. If no one is linking to a webpage, it goes into obscurity.

We can complain about these facts, or we can use it to our benefit.

Here's how I choose to interpret it:

We are liberated to create and share as much as we'd like.

We can let go of any fear of making mediocre content.

Since quantity leads to quality, what makes sense is to **create more.** Keep creating, and I promise *some* of your stuff will be exceptional. The rest? It merely gave you practice.

Share more of your thoughts. It works your muscles of expression and reveals which of your many ideas happens to also resonate with your audience.

Write more about your framework. Talk about the "aha!" moments in your work with clients. Post occasional invitations to work with your business.

Whatever is good will spread. Whatever isn't, will quickly be forgotten.

Always remember: what is "good" content is not up to *you* to decide. Your role is to create and share. It's your audience's role to decide whether something is worth remembering.

What's worthwhile will get above-average likes, comments, and shares.

If you don't see much engagement -- (if you get silence) -- then it's your audience's gentle feedback that they didn't think much of it... no matter how important it felt to you.

Take a pause, and simply move on to create and share the next thing.

(The other possibility, if you *always* get silence, is that you haven't reached the right audience. Try another audience to share your content with.)

Having created thousands of pieces of content, there have been many that I felt were really important... but you (my audience) didn't think so!

So there was silence. I don't blame anyone. It's just the illusion that I as a creator experience: *because I spent time creating something, it feels important to me.*

You'll experience the same bias: the more effort you spend in recording a video or writing an article, the more important it'll feel to you.

This is why I teach the 3 stages of content. Spend *as little effort as possible* in putting out your ideas. If an idea resonates with your audience, **then** it's worth additional effort to improve upon it.

When a piece of content is finally loved by your audience, the algorithms will generously show it to others who weren't part of your audience... and then new people will discover you.

Most of the time, however -- and this is simply statistics! -- your content *won't* go viral. It will be seen by only a few of your biggest fans. And that's ok.

Remember: when you create, you win, no matter what.

Either your audience will love it... or they won't, and you simply got practice expressing your voice and clarifying your message.

As long as you create from an energetic space (or attitude) of service and expression, then you are growing, no matter what.

If you want to increase your skills and opportunities, simply create and share more content!

To watch the companion video or comment on this chapter, go here: http://bit.ly/acmv2c17

Start Building An Audience Now — Even If You Have Nothing To Sell

A regret for many entrepreneurs is that they didn't start building their audience sooner.

If you *might* want to start a business one day, I recommend that you start growing your audience **now**.

For audience building, it *does not* matter if you don't have clarity about what you'll focus your business on. Of course message clarity can help, but you can still build an audience based on your personal brand first.

Start by talking about *any* of your authentic interests—you'll end up with an audience who like your personality, values, and align with you on some of your interests—and that's better than having no audience at all.

How to Start?

- Whenever you come across an idea that is interesting or helpful to you, share it on social media (whichever platform you use).
- As you read an article or book that you find interesting, write a quick summary of it and post it on social media.
- As you watch and find a video you really like, share it, and say why it's worth watching.
- If there's something you disagree with, be sure to say why—start practicing your muscles of saying *what you believe*.
- If you have a sense of what your passion is, or what your future business *might* be, start a Facebook Business Page right

away. Just use your own name—build your personal brand—you can always change your Page Name later.

Whatever You Do, Start Now.

Which social media platform to choose? Start with the one you personally enjoy using. I recommend choosing between Facebook, Youtube, or Instagram. Any of these are big enough to build you an audience.

Build your audience continuously by creating authentic content.

Then, when you are ready in the future to promote some kind of product, service, or cause, you will have an audience to receive it, people who already know and trust you.

The Fantasy of "Instant Promotion"

Many business owners have the fantasy of "instant promotion"—that they're able to gain buyers for their product/service right away... when they have *no* audience.

Instant promotion *only* works in one of these two cases:

- You sell something mainstream: a product that many people already buy, and are looking for a business they trust, e.g. graphic design.
- Or you have the means to start with a large advertising budget, e.g. $1,000 per month.

If instead, you are selling something that not a lot of people you personally know are buying (coaching, counseling, alternative healing, etc.) and you only have maybe $50/month advertising budget, then you need to start building your audience as soon as possible.

Don't expect to wait until you're "ready" to sell something, and then "just" post it on Facebook or tweet it out, and expect clients to sign up.

The harsh truth is, if no one knows who you are, no one's going to buy from you.

Good Copywriting and Branding Won't Save You Either

Maybe you think—*"I'll just hire a copywriter or marketing expert. They'll help me create amazing messaging and branding…"*—this is yet another fantasy.

I've seen it too often: even *amazing* messaging and branding are often a huge disappointment and a waste of money, if it is not tied to a relationship with an existing audience.

If, however, you build an audience **first**, get to know them, and base your marketing message on *what you've observed about them* then you will be able to get clients quickly and without manipulative marketing.

What It Means To "Have An Audience"

1. You've been sharing helpful content on social media, and you notice that you have several dozen people who engage with your content on a regular basis.

2. Or you're a good networker, and have dozens of friends and colleagues that you have supportive relationships with, who are likely to promote your business when it's time to do so.

Ideally you have both, but start at least one of these efforts - sharing content or networking - as soon as possible. Through the process of authentic content marketing, you will build an audience around your "personal brand" (your name, thoughts, your authentic style), that will give you the flexibility to pivot to having any kind of business you want in the future.

Don't Wait Until You Figure Out What Your Niche Is

This is a fantasy:

- *Figure out your business idea or niche → Promote it and get customers*
  (Again, this doesn't work unless you have a mainstream service or a large advertising budget.)

Authentic business success works more like this:

* Build an audience → Get to know them → Create your marketing message and offerings → Get customers/clients

Before you figure out your niche, start creating a network/audience for your personal brand **now**.

In The Not-Too-Distant Future…

Given the rapid growth of artificial intelligence and automation, humans will have an increasingly hard time finding a job.

This is not happening in the distant future… you'll see major changes in the next 10 years.

If you develop entrepreneurial skills, and build your own audience, you'll be in a much better position to create your own livelihood, your own meaningful work, instead of hoping someone will give you a job.

For everyone who wants meaningful work in the future, it is imperative to start building one's own audience now.

When's the best time to have planted a tree?

10 years ago.

When's the next best time?

Today.

This is true of your personal brand as well.

Your audience and brand don't have to take 10 years to build. But if you start today, you will be in a better position one year from now.

Whether or not you have a business already, start growing your audience now.

To watch the companion video or comment on this chapter, go here: http://bit.ly/acmv2c18

Let's Support Small Creators!

The 1% own more than half of the entire world's wealth.

The accumulation of assets in the hands of the few erodes democracy, as societal power becomes concentrated in the hands of a few.

Knowing this, anything we can do to support small businesses will not just help entrepreneurs survive, but will support more democracy, creativity, and true livelihood in the world.

Similarly, the 1% most famous people own a huge share of the consumer's attention.

Influencers like Gary Vaynurchuk, Marie Forleo, Brene Brown, Joe Dispenza, and other celebrities own a *disproportionate* amount of our content consumption time.

The accumulation of attention in the hands of a few will erode the diversity of creativity, true livelihood, and authentic business...

Where Is Your Attention Going?

Attention, like time, is limited. We ought to be more mindful of where it goes.

I encourage you to start giving 10% or more of your attention each day to small creators: bloggers, video makers, podcasts, websites, or social media pages that get few comments on their content.

(By "small creator" I mean "small business", not that they are small thinkers! Their hearts are far bigger than their current numbers.)

You can still spend the vast majority of your media time giving attention to big influencers, thought leaders, and to Netflix and the major studios. Let's just mindfully spend 10% of our content consumption time gifting a bit of our attention to small creators because it makes such a life-changing difference for them... and for us!

When **your** comment is *one of the only comments* that a small creator gets, for them it feels like finding water in a dry desert.

It feeds their hearts and supports their passion.

Your supportive comment helps them power through the many times they experience silence (zero feedback).

On the other hand, when you "like" or comment on a **popular** creator's post, it's like a drop in the ocean, making almost no difference to them.

Let's be more mindful content consumers, and care for our fellow small creators!

There are three things we can do in our 10% time…

1. Engage.

Find a small creator (blog, Facebook page, Medium page, Youtube channel, Podcast, Instagram, Twitter account, etc.)

Look for a post that has few comments, and be one of the only commenters for them. It makes such a difference… Your comment could inspire days of creative energy!

What to say in your comment?

- **What you like** about that piece of content. Even if it's not the most brilliant thing you've ever seen, there's still something good about it — call out the good. If it's a piece of writing, highlight a sentence or paragraph. If it's a video, say what you liked about their presence or message.

- **What can be improved** — it's super helpful for content creators to get feedback about how they can improve. You might want to do this privately, though. *Praise publicly, critique privately.* Tell them what you'd love for them to create content on… what topics interest you, that might be in their field of expertise?

If you really liked that piece of content, go the extra mile and **share it forward!**

2. Buy.

Each week or month, find a small creator whose products you'd like to support, and spend some money with them.

Your purchase might be the only one they have that whole week!

They put their heart and soul into creating a product, and it makes such a difference when someone votes "yes" by purchasing it.

And don't just buy it. Use the product :)

3. Review.

Finally, you can make the biggest difference when you post a positive review of their product or service.

For your review, think about the potential buyer: what will help them make a buying decision? They want the honest opinion of someone who's actually used the product. When you were initially looking at the product, what would you have wanted to know?

(For any negative feedback, send it to the creator privately, with a spirit of kindness and an intention to help make the product better.)

After writing your review, here are some places to post it:

- Find their Facebook Business Page and if there's a Reviews tab there, use that.
- Find their profile on Linkedin and write them a recommendation. Most Linkedin profiles have no recommendations or maybe a few. Yours will make a real difference to their profile!
- Search their name on Google Maps and, if they have a business profile there, review them.
- Search for them on Yelp and, if they have a page there, review them.

Email them the review and give them permission to use it anywhere!

They might feature your testimonial on their website and therefore, you could literally be helping their business for years to come.

Start With Your Friends

Are any of them trying to be consistent with their content? Engage with their content, especially the ones with few comments. Then, do the other actions if you can: Buy and Review. They will be so grateful you did!

Facebook tip: use your friend lists to make your social media caring easier.

The simple act of redirecting just 10% of your content consumption time, can bring gratitude and hope to your fellow small creators everyday.

To watch the companion video or comment on this chapter, go here: http://bit.ly/acmv2c19

You Are Perfect Enough. You Know Enough. You Are Ready.

Are you hesitant about putting your work out there?

What if you get clients that you can't help?

What if there's another course that will finally give you the tools you need?

If you're saying 'Yes' to any of the above, you are under the illusion that there is an end or final destination to the acquisition of knowledge, skills, and experience.

There isn't.

Forever, there will be more knowledge out there that feels like it could be "the key". Even if you get multiple Ph.D.s, you'll still feel like you don't know enough. (Actually, with more knowledge, it's likely you'll struggle even more to organize all the learned information into a coherent framework.)

No matter how much you learn cognitively, you still won't feel ready to get out there. What's the most reliable way to feel more ready?

To learn through actual experiences.

Everybody gets clients that intimidate them. Every expert sometimes feels like they don't have the right answers.

You simply need to experience more of the real work.

- Take on that client that scares you.
- Teach that topic you've been studying but not sure you're an expert in.
- Create content on the things you're learning about.

By putting yourself out there, you will soon discover that some people value your work and truly appreciate what you already know. Not everyone will praise you, but you don't need everyone.

You just need to observe who does indeed appreciate your work at this stage -- for they are your ideal clients **now**.

In the beginning of my coaching career, I was fortunate to meet a leader of a large organization who believed that I had some productivity skills that would be helpful to him. I felt intimidated by his great leadership experience. I didn't feel "ready". But he clearly saw something I could offer him, some skill that was so natural for me that I didn't think it was a big deal.

It's the same with you. You already know enough to help a lot of people.

Stop asking yourself whether you're ready. Instead, ask whether you see people struggling with something you already know. What have you thought a lot more about than the average person? Use this as a starting point.

You **don't** have to be fully integrated with that knowledge or tool, to be able to coach or teach. It can still be a real and ongoing issue in your own life, but at least you're more aware of it than the average person, and you have some tools for solving the problem, even if you haven't fully solved it for yourself.

Here's the most interesting part -- it's actually **better** for the client that you haven't fully moved beyond the issue.

Why?

Because the more you can viscerally relate to them, the more they will feel seen and heard... and feeling understood makes them more open to your support!

Have you heard of the curse of knowledge? It's where the expert has solved the problem and gotten so far beyond the original state of mind, that it's hard for them to put themselves in the client's current experience.

While you are still struggling with the very issues you want to help people with, it's so important for you to journal about:

- those struggles
- the various angles of it and situations where it comes into play
- your reflections on it
- the insights or tools that are helping you as you work on yourself.

It is such a precious time now, because you will eventually move beyond these issues and forget what it felt like. Trust me, you will forget! Write (or record) copiously now.

While you're going through it now, share your writing publicly, as much as you can. (I call it public journaling.) Your writing will connect with others who are dealing with your issues (these are your kindred spirits, or your potential clients!) and they will appreciate your awareness and insights.

No one else but an experiencer like you can write (or record) about the struggles in a real way. Share what reflections and tools are helping you. By doing this, you're creating true credibility.

Demonstrating that you really understand what they're going through, may actually be the most helpful thing to your clients. Given that you're just one or a few steps ahead of them, you can truly hold their hand and help them forward.

To watch the companion video or comment on this chapter, go here: http://bit.ly/acmv2c20

Acknowledgements

These kind souls helped me edit this book: Angie Evans, Brian Smith, Heather Tobin, Joselito Laudencia, Alexandra Madsen, and Leah Cooper.

Thank you!

I also offer my thanks to my Facebook Page commenters who gave their impressions of the book's cover designs.

Especially to Chris Adel, Philippa Castell, Birgit Olzem, and Todd Ringness for taking the initiative to submit some designs! You can see what they submitted here.

To all of my clients: I deeply honor the work you do. Your dedication to continue improving your authentic business is inspiring.

To my students: Thank you for your sincere engagement with the course material and your thoughtful questions. You are helping me create better courses.

To those who watch my videos and read my posts: Each time I see your views, likes and comments, it encourages and inspires me to become more effective in serving you.

Your questions and comments have helped to make the content of this book.

To my affiliate community: I'm grateful for your trust in my ability to help those you refer to me. I'll continue to do my best to make you proud!

Lastly, to my wife: My heartfelt gratitude for your loyal support and love. You provide an amazing foundation for my joyful productivity.

About The Author

Since 2009, George Kao has been a marketing mentor, consultant, and coach to thousands of small business owners, speakers, and authors.

George's mission is to raise the marketing effectiveness of those who prioritize integrity, compassion, and generosity in their business.

George teaches online courses about authentic online marketing, including Facebook Advertising, Google Advertising, authentic content creation, defining your core message, how to create and market courses, and joyful productivity. You can find all his current courses at www.GeorgeKao.com/Workshops

To receive a regular email newsletter with George's best articles, visit www.GeorgeKao.com/Newsletter

www.ingramcontent.com/pod-product-compliance
Lightning Source LLC
Chambersburg PA
CBHW030451220526
45464CB00006B/2496